THE NEGOTIATOR'S POCKETBOOK

By Patrick Forsyth
Drawings by Phil Hailstone

"A very practical book, not just giving you the key principles, but full of tips which can help you feel like an expert and negotiate with confidence."
Robin Birn, Managing Director, Strategy, Research and Action Ltd

"A ready reminder of those skills and techniques any negotiator needs, presented in a witty and easy to read form."
Anthony Skinner, OSM Ltd

CONTENTS

1 INTRODUCTION

When a man tells me he is going to put all his cards on the table, I always look up his sleeve.

Lord Hore-Belisha

A USEFUL SKILL

Negotiation can smooth relations. It can save you time, money, aggravation and 'face' ..... or gain you a positive advantage.

But there is a catch (isn't there always?). Negotiation is a complex process. It involves learning some skills and some practice.

This pocketbook is designed to help you do better and achieve more in a variety of negotiating situations. I want you to buy it. You want to be a better negotiator. Buy it (and read it) and we both get what we want. Is it a deal?

DEFINITION

Negotiation takes place when two people (or more), with differing views, come together to attempt to reach agreement on some issue. This may be a one-off event or part of an on-going relationship.

It is a form of communication known as persuasive communication. In a word, bargaining.

Persuasive communication is about getting what you want. Negotiation is about getting the best possible deal: that is, getting what you want in the best possible way.

INTRODUCTION

COMMUNICATION OVERLAP

Persuasiveness and negotiation are forms of communication. Like all forms of communication, they are never as simple as they seem. To keep this clear, think of them as an overlapping process:

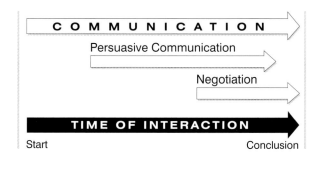

NEGOTIATION: 2 TYPES

1. DISTRIBUTIVE

Sometimes called 'win/lose' negotiation, **distributive** negotiation arises when the parties are in conflict. Each sees the objective as beating the other. This leads to negative tactics and makes confrontation more likely, with a satisfactory conclusion more difficult to obtain than in more mutually positive encounters.

NEGOTIATION: 2 TYPES

2. INTEGRATIVE

Sometimes called 'win/win' negotiation, **integrative** negotiation arises when the parties see the aim as gaining agreement. Through collaboration and compromise this approach is more likely to lead to an outcome that is acceptable to both parties.

INTRODUCTION

USES OF NEGOTIATION

Negotiation has many purposes, for example in:

- Persuasive communication and selling
- Purchasing
- Dealing with staff
- Arbitration
- Many business or personal transactions, from buying a computer to agreeing when and where to meet for dinner

Everything is negotiable – everyone is a negotiator.

FUNDAMENTALS OF NEGOTIATION

CORE OF THE PROCESS

Negotiation is the process of:

- Identifying
- Debating
- Arranging, and
- Agreeing to **terms**

The different elements are referred to, in the jargon of negotiation, as **variables** or **concessions**.

Negotiation demands the **trading** of concessions, whether these are tangible or intangible, major or minor.

Remember, everything is potentially negotiable.

CORE OF THE PROCESS

WHAT EXACTLY ARE VARIABLES?

They will include a host of things, such as:

- price	- follow up
- discount	- service
- delivery	- timing
- payment terms	- schedules
- people	- urgency
- extras	- guarantees
- contracts	- conditions
- terms	- place
- documentation	- options

Always make sure you overlook nothing. What else would you add to this list?

FUNDAMENTALS OF NEGOTIATION

POWER TO INFLUENCE

What gives a negotiator power to influence events?

- **Promise of reward**
  You can provide something the other side wants, so they have to listen

- **Threat of punishment**
  The apparent intention **not** to provide something the other side wants

- **Legitimacy**
  Factual evidence: something that clearly weighs in the argument

- **Bogeys**
  Something fielded specifically to give you an edge (such as sympathy)

Never underestimate or overestimate your power or theirs.

FUNDAMENTALS OF NEGOTIATION

POWER TO INFLUENCE

There is one additional source of power, one of major significance: **confidence.**

If others believe they are dealing with someone confident, competent, organised and efficient then they may be less certain of their own position.

Confidence comes from preparation, a structured approach, knowledge, and **belief.** Convince yourself of your confidence and you will convince them that you are a power to be reckoned with.

As the saying goes:
'If you can fake confidence,
then everything else is easy!'

FUNDAMENTALS OF NEGOTIATION

FOUR ESSENTIAL RULES

1. AIM HIGH

Aim for the best deal. You can always trade down but it is more difficult to trade up.

Now in your mind divide the variables into:

- **Musts:** what you feel you must take from the table if the deal is going to be acceptable to you
- **Ideals:** what you prefer to achieve to make the 'ideal' deal
- **Loss leaders:** those things you are prepared to trade in order to close a deal (even if you would prefer to keep them)

Be realistic. Negotiating is about trading concessions, so you MUST have items in all three categories.

FOUR ESSENTIAL RULES

2. GET THE OTHER PERSON'S 'SHOPPING LIST'

The more you know about the other side the better you will do.

How much can you intelligently infer or anticipate about the views of the other side?

To find out and keep **both** sides of the discussion in mind, use:

- Preparation
- Prior knowledge
- Experience
- Questioning skills

FUNDAMENTALS OF NEGOTIATION

FOUR ESSENTIAL RULES

3. KEEP THE WHOLE PACKAGE IN MIND

Do not underestimate the complexity of negotiating.

It is the interrelationship between all the elements that makes negotiation work. You need to keep all the elements in mind **all the time.**

4. KEEP SEARCHING FOR VARIABLES

Remain flexible.

Do not wear your plan or initial intentions like a strait-jacket.

Everything is negotiable **and a few more things besides.** Good negotiators are quick on their feet.

FUNDAMENTALS OF NEGOTIATION

THE POINT OF BALANCE

Negotiation assumes that a point of balance will be found.

Participants start at opposite ends of the scale but must move towards something they both regard as an acceptable deal.

A range of solutions may be possible at, or near, the centre.

Negotiation is a to and fro process that moves up and down the line.

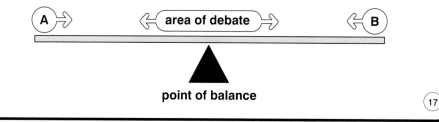

point of balance

BRIDGES OF RAPPORT

People are more likely to see your point of view if they can relate to it. Bridges make this possible. For example:

- Open the discussion on a neutral subject to allay any hostility, obtain initial agreement, and engage the other person in conversation

- When holding back, assure the other party that you will make every effort to come to a mutually agreeable outcome

- Demonstrate respect for the other person and for the process. For example, pay a compliment about a contribution that has been useful

- Refer back to agreement: reinforce your persuasion by linking to the other person's needs (what it is they need from you)

- Make it clear what all the component parts of your offer are worth to them

- Try to present a clear explanation or justification for any complex issues

TRADING CONCESSIONS

1. NEVER <u>GIVE</u> A CONCESSION; <u>TRADE</u> IT RELUCTANTLY

The first part of this rule is important because the number of variables is finite and you want your share. The second part is also crucial because perception is as important as fact: we must appear to be driving a hard bargain.

This is the 'if ..... /then' approach.

TRADING CONCESSIONS

2. OPTIMISE <u>YOUR</u> CONCESSIONS

Build up the value and significance of anything you offer to trade by:

- Stressing the cost (financial or otherwise) to you ('Well, I could do that but it would involve a lot more work')

- Exaggerating – credibly. Do not overstate and, if possible, provide evidence ('Well, I could do that but it would involve at least twice as much work; I have just been through …..')

- Referring to a major problem that your concession would solve ('Well, I suppose if I were to agree, it would remove the need for you to …..')

- Implying that it is an exceptional concession ('I would never normally do this, but …..')

- Implying that it is not only exceptional but beyond the call of duty ('I really don't know what my boss will say but …..')

Maximise the **perceived** value of everything you offer.

TRADING CONCESSIONS

3. MINIMISE THEIR CONCESSIONS

Reduce the value that the other party puts on anything offered to you:

- Do not overdo the thanks. Avoid a profuse 'Thank you so much' but be brief, even dismissive, 'Thanks' (your tone of voice is as important as the phrase you use)

- Depreciate, or belittle, the value of the other person's concession ('Right, that's a small step forward, I guess')

- Amortise the concession where appropriate. Divide it into smaller units that will sound less impressive ('Well, at least that saves me X every month' rather than quoting the total figure)

- Treat concessions as given but don't put a value on them. A brief acknowledgement may be all that is necessary ('Right, let's do it that way')

TRADING CONCESSIONS

3. MINIMISE <u>THEIR</u> CONCESSIONS (cont'd)

- Take concessions for granted. In other words, treat them as if they were always a foregone conclusion ('Fine, I would certainly expect that')
- Devalue by implying that you already have what is being offered ('OK, though I have already .....')
- Accept but imply that you are doing the other person a favour ('I don't really need that, but let's arrange things that way if it helps')
- Link value to time by suggesting that it is now not worth what is implied ('Well, that helps a little but it is not of major importance now that we have done .....')
- Deny any value ('That really doesn't help')

MONEY MATTERS

One of the variables in many negotiations is financial (price, margins, discounts, fees, costs, profit).

The good negotiator is financially numerate, does his/her financial homework and can work a calculator!

MONEY MATTERS

MARGINS

In selling, remember that if volume remains constant, a change in price will directly – and perhaps dramatically – affect profits, e.g.:

		5% Price Increase	5% Price Reduction
Sales	100,000	105,000	95,000
Variable Costs	**60,000**	**60,000**	**60,000**
Gross Profit	40,000	45,000	35,000
Fixed Costs	**25,000**	**25,000**	**25,000**
Net Profit	15,000	20,000	10,000

Small changes in price have a dramatic effect on profits.

PREPARATION

PREPARATION

RULE 1: DO IT

You cannot guarantee success if negotiation is conducted
'off the top of your head'. There is an old saying

*'The only place where success comes before work
is in the dictionary'.*

Successful negotiators do their homework.

SEVEN KEY STAGES

1. SET CLEAR OBJECTIVES

You should be clear what you want to achieve and have a firm opinion of what the other party wants from the negotiation.

But you should be able to state your objectives in terms of the needs of the other party:

Example:

You want to increase your prices by 5% So, the other person must be persuaded to be content to purchase at **only** 5% more than last year

This difference of perception must pervade the conversation.

SEVEN KEY STAGES

1. SET CLEAR OBJECTIVES (cont'd)

Objectives should be **SMART.**

S pecific

M easurable

A chievable

R ealistic

T imed

Only then can achievement of them be monitored usefully.

PREPARATION

SEVEN KEY STAGES

2. IDENTIFY THE OTHER PERSON'S NEEDS

This stage may have its roots further back, for instance at the selling stage.

Ask yourself questions about the other people:

- What are their key needs?
- What are their financial needs?
- What problems do they have?
- What priorities do they have?
- What alternatives do they see?
- What do you know about the nature of the people?
- How will decisions be made?
- How will all this relate to what you intend?

Never stop asking, assembling and analysing information.

Information is power.

SEVEN KEY STAGES

3. IDENTIFY NEGOTIATION ELEMENTS

Do not assume that certain areas will be excluded. Remember, the vital principle: look for variables (see page 11). Start by identifying all possible variables NOW before the meeting.

List them, dividing them into:

- Quantifiable elements (e.g.: price/costs)
- Unquantifiable elements (e.g.: service/design)

SEVEN KEY STAGES

3. IDENTIFY NEGOTIATION ELEMENTS (cont'd)

Having listed the anticipated elements, consider which are:

- Essential
- Attractive extras
- Relatively unimportant

Think about the importance you **and** the other party will give to these elements.
Watch out: what you consider normal or routine may be considered exceptional by
the other person.

Then, for each element, ask yourself:

- What is my best estimate of the likely point of agreement?
- What is the lowest/worst position I can accept?
- How will the other party see this?

SEVEN KEY STAGES

4. DECIDE ON CONCESSIONS AND THEIR VALUE

What are you prepared to trade?　　　⇨　　What will they want?

What will you give?　　　⇨　　What will they concede?

Put a cost against everything you may need to trade. Some things are clearly costed; others need more scrutiny (for example, 'What is the cost of delay?').

Think through the balance of options as in this sales example:

Concessions from you:　　　　　　　**Concessions from customer:**

Reduce price to £10.00　　　⇨　　Increase volume to 1150 units

Reduce price to £9.50　　　⇨　　Increase volume to 1320 units

Reduce price to £9.00　　　⇨　　Increase volume to 1560 units

PREPARATION

SEVEN KEY STAGES

5. CALCULATE OVERALL EFFECT OF PACKAGE

- Add up the elements you may need to trade
- If the total 'cost' is too high, reconsider the individual elements in order to assemble a better package

At this stage you should have the basis of a range of deals. One end of this range will be the ideal, the other end will be the minimum acceptable. The strategy is to end up as far towards the ideal as possible, bearing in mind that some form of compromise is almost always necessary.

With this picture clearly in your mind, you will be able to make the necessary decisions promptly as discussions proceed.

SEVEN KEY STAGES

6. PREPARE YOUR STANCES

The process of negotiation is like a seesaw:

- The likely point of agreement is the point of balance
- On either side of the point of balance, there is the gap you need to close
- Aim to start your side of the discussions so that you are approximately in balance with the other party

EXAMPLE (price negotiation)

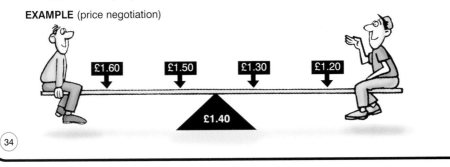

SEVEN KEY STAGES

6. PREPARE YOUR STANCES (cont'd)

The specific stages of preparing your stances are:

1. Look at the total package and try to estimate where you think the other person will start

2. Make the opposite point of balance your overall starting point

3. Consider each individual item in turn

4. Estimate, for each one, where the other person is likely to start

5. Determine where you will start, paying attention to:
   - the individual points of balance
   - the overall package
   - the different emphasis to give to each element depending on its importance to each side
   - the fall-back positions

SEVEN KEY STAGES

7. PREPARE TO CONDUCT MEETING

You will need to be open-minded and prepared to trade. Remember, the skill of negotiating is to trade **values rather than costs**. So:

- Prepare what you can **give**:
  - How can you add value to it?
  - How can you suggest how costly it is to you?

- Prepare for what you are **likely to be offered**:
  - How can you reduce its apparent value to you?
  - Can you suggest how little it has cost the other party?
  - Do you know the cost of accepting it?

- Prepare where you can **devalue**:
  - The costs to the other party.
  - The value to you of any concessions.

- Prepare where you can **increase the value** of:
  - Concessions you offer.
  - The perceived cost of your giving them.

Keep the overall situation in mind.

GROUP NEGOTIATIONS

Some negotiation meetings involve a number of people, sometimes on both sides. This inevitably increases the complexities involved.

Preparation in such circumstances must always **include** clear allocation of roles beforehand about:

- Who will lead
- Who will do what, and
- How you will achieve a smooth (seamless) handover during the course of the meeting

No negotiation is likely to be successful if members of the team are falling over each other's feet.

REHEARSAL

The ultimate form of preparation is **rehearsal.**

Remember, there may be a great deal hanging on the outcome of your negotiation.
It is worth the time and effort of trying it out in advance and fine tuning it based on feedback. So:

- Practise in front of the mirror
- Use a tape recorder
- Try it on a friend or colleague
- Role-play it, informally, with someone
- Try it on the dog!

TEN TECHNIQUES TO KEEP AHEAD

1. USE SILENCE

Saying nothing can be as powerful as saying something, provided it is used at the right time and in the right way. Most people are quickly embarrassed by silence. It usually requires a conscious effort to maintain one, but can be very useful.

- If you cannot optimise or minimise, silence can imply you are non-committal.

- A silence can imply certainty on your part (and prompt uncertainty in the other person). Thus, having made a clear suggestion – 'So what do you think?' – wait. (Do not allow the pause to push you into diluting what you have just said.)

2. SUMMARISE FREQUENTLY

Negotiations are, by definition, complex. They involve juggling a number of variables. It is easy to lose the thread, so never be afraid to summarise. For example, summarise where you have got so far or recap where you left one aspect of the discussion.

Linking this to using 'suppose' or 'if' keeps the conversation organised and allows you to explore possibilities without committing yourself. ('Right, we have agreed that we need to resolve cost, delivery and timing, now if ….. then …..')

TEN TECHNIQUES TO KEEP AHEAD

3. TAKE NOTES

Keep track of complex negotiations throughout their course. While the formality of certain meetings is inappropriate for note-taking, you must keep track. Remember, information is power. Never leave yourself groping ('What did we say about so and so?').

Not only will taking notes prevent you being caught out on something that you cannot remember, but making them or checking them can have another advantage. It gives you time to think: either as you say 'Let me make a note of that' (and obviously do so) or when you say 'Let me check what we agreed about that'.

The brain works a lot faster than the pen. It is sometimes surprising just how much thought you can bring to bear as you write down two or three (sometimes irrelevant) words on your pad.

4. PROMOTE A GOOD FEELING

Negotiation tends to build up agreement progressively. As you proceed, make sure you emphasise that each stage is good, preferably for both parties but particularly for the other person.

Phrases like 'That's a good arrangement', 'That will work well',
'That's fair', 'That's a good suggestion, let's do it
that way', help the agreement build.

Agreement

Start

'ok'   'good'   'right'

NEGOTIATION

5. READ BETWEEN THE LINES

Remember, negotiation is essentially an adversarial process. Both parties want the best for themselves, and the only signs of approaching traps (or success) come via the other person. Particularly watch for danger phrases: those that often mean something other than what they seem, or mean the opposite of what they say. For example:

- 'You're a reasonable fellow' (*Meaning* 'I am')
- 'That's much fairer to us both' (*Meaning* 'Especially to me')
- 'It looks like we are almost there' (*Meaning* 'There is something else I want')
- 'Now, we only need to clear up a couple of minor details' (*Minor? For whom?*)
- 'That's everything' (*Followed by* '….. except for one more thing …..')

6. MAINTAIN NEUTRALITY

Maintain neutrality as much, and for as long, as possible. Negotiation works best as a balancing exercise. If one party throws the whole basis of discussion up in the air – 'It is not as good as the other deal I am considering' – this can take things back to square one.

Keep the whole process focused on negotiating arrangements, rather than questioning whether there is a deal to be done. If it is necessary to go back to the offer itself, so be it; but that is persuasive communication. Negotiation must concentrate on terms and conditions.

7. KEEP THINKING

Keep thinking – and build in time to think. The power of silence has already been mentioned: use it to think ahead. Use note-taking in the same way.

Use any delaying tactic – working something out on a calculator or making a telephone call – but do not let your mouth get ahead of your brain.

Of course, if you can encourage the other person to do just that, so much the better.

8. HOLD YOUR FIRE

Try not to make an offer, certainly not a final offer, until everything that needs negotiating is out on the table.

This may need no more than a question like, 'Yes, I am sure I can help there; now, is there anything else that you want to consider?'. If necessary, ask more questions and keep pursuing the point.

9. DON'T GET HUNG UP ON DEADLINES

There is an old saying that there has not been a deadline in history that wasn't negotiable.

All aspects of timing are variables:

- How long will things take? (Duration)
- When will they happen? (Time frame)
- All at once? (Prioritisation)

Keep this in mind throughout the negotiation process.

10. REMEMBER: CONSTRAINTS & VARIABLES ARE INTERCHANGEABLE

Almost anything the other side presents as fixed can be made into a variable.

Fixed is as likely to mean not wanting to negotiate as not able to be negotiated.

FINAL ADVICE

Run the conversation **you** want, in a way that the **other person** finds acceptable/professional.

Getting off to a good start sets the process in motion. Fine tuning as you go along keeps you progressing as you want.

MANAGING THE PROCESS

HAVE AND USE A PLAN

Always know what you are going to do and plan how you are going to do it. This should include getting any necessary prior agreements or authority to act from others on your side. (You lose impetus and 'face' if you break off halfway through to take advice or instruction).

Let your plan act like a route map, not a strait-jacket.

You cannot predict exactly how things will go, but you can greatly assist the process by:

- Anticipating the stages as much as possible
- Having in mind what you want to do
- Recognising when things are getting off track
- Working consciously with the whole process

This does not mean you must adopt a 'scripted' or parrotlike approach, but that you intend, and plan, to control the direction of the conversation towards a specific objective.

HAVE AND USE A PLAN

KEEP ON TRACK

It may help to think of this graphically, as the captain of a sailing yacht, proceeding across the open sea, subject to the impact of wind and weather. The captain might take a number of courses but, by having a clear picture of the destination and by imagining a straight line towards it, he will be able to make corrections and keep on track.

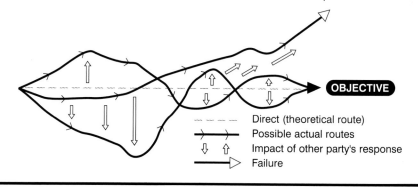

OBJECTIVE

‑ ‑ ‑   Direct (theoretical route)

——▶   Possible actual routes

⇩ ⇧   Impact of other party's response

▷   Failure

CREATE PHYSICAL ADVANTAGE

All things being equal, sit where you can see (and hear) everyone else and be seen clearly yourself. This is particularly relevant if discussions involve a number of people.

If possible, it is best to conduct the meeting on your own territory. You will feel more in control (they less so) and you have all your information and support close by.

KEEP NUMBERS DOWN

The fewer people involved the better.
Certainly, less time is taken to
reach an agreement.

In particular, resist being outnumbered.

COMMUNICATE CLEARLY

Negotiation is complex and problems will inevitably arise if communication is unclear.
Make what you say:

- Understandable
- Attractive
- Credible

Be sure that particular points of issue or agreement are:

- Succinct
- Specific
- Accurate

By doing so, it won't become necessary to keep re-defining meaning during discussion.
Moreover, those items progressively agreed to are clearly noted and will be represented
accurately in any ensuing contract.

DELIVER

Throughout the proceedings:

Always promise only what you can deliver

Good long-term relationships are
founded on mutually fulfilled
promises. Failure to deliver – even
on one small point – can damage
a person's credibility irretrievably.

Never over-sell your case.

TO AND FRO DISCUSSION (1)

- Try to encourage the other people to do most of the talking early on but do not avoid their questions
- Respond to their stances by:
  - accepting, but persuading them that the negatives outweigh the positives
  - accepting, but going back to basic problems and suggesting alternatives
  - ignoring, and presenting your own stance
  - taking the opposite view
  - accepting, and using a 'let's suppose' technique to present alternatives

Focus attention on moving closer to your ideal position.

TO AND FRO DISCUSSION (2)

- Present your own stances by:
  - taking an exaggerated view
  - taking the actual stance (especially when your case is strong)
  - indicating initial acceptance
  - agreeing with elements of both parties' position

This will shift attention away from their position and focus attention on yours.

Overall, move the discussion from opening stances to a clear statement of actual stances.

And, as you proceed, successfully 'save face' for the other person. Do not use any version of 'gotcha'.

NOTES

INTERPERSONAL BEHAVIOUR

INTERPERSONAL BEHAVIOUR

'READING' THE SITUATION

Negotiation is not simply a matter of techniques, although these are important. It is also dependent on 'reading' the other people involved. Key behavioural tactics include:

- 'Reading between the lines' to seek the real meaning

- Listening actively

- Observing body language

- Reacting to all the rituals of the process to secure the best possible deal

HOW YOU COME ACROSS

Your manner must be persuasive yet always acceptable. Two factors help create the correct manner:

- **Projection** - the way you are perceived by others and, in particular, the confidence, credibility and 'clout' with which you come across
- **Empathy** - the ability to demonstrate that you see the other person's point of view

Four types of communicator
(see next page for definitions)

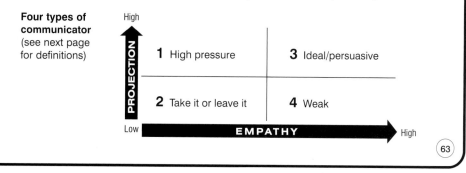

63

HOW YOU COME ACROSS
FOUR TYPES OF COMMUNICATOR

High pressure communicators are over-aggressive and insensitive. They may feel they can win the argument but, in fact, their projection, without empathy, becomes self-defeating and turns people off. The archetypal high-pressure person is the popular image of a used car salesperson.

Take-it-or-leave-it communicators have little interest in either the other person or, curiously, their own ideas. A lack of commitment to the whole process tends to let things run into the ground. The archetypal take-it-or-leave-it person is the kind of unhelpful customer service representative with whom most of us are all too familiar.

Weak communicators are the sort of which it is said, disparagingly, 'They mean well'. And so they do: they are sensitive to the other person, come over as essentially nice, but take the side of the listener so much on occasion that persuasion vanishes and they achieve no commitment.

Ideal/persuasive communicators are seen as having a creative understanding of the listener, being well informed, and producing both agreement and commitment to the satisfaction of both sides. Being outwardly empathetic to the other person's point of view is crucial.

Maintain a balanced overall approach.

INTERPERSONAL BEHAVIOUR

VERBAL SIGNS

It is not what is said that is significant, it is what is **really** meant. Consider these 'hidden signals:'

One party says:	And means:
'We would find it extremely difficult to meet the deadline'	'If we do meet it, it must be worth something'
'Our organisation is not set up to cope with that'	'So, if we do, consider it a real favour'
'I do not have the authority to arrange .....'	'But someone else does'
'It is not our normal practice to do that'	'I could make an exception'
'I never negotiate on price'	'If you want to, you start'
'We can discuss that point'	'It is negotiable'
'We are not prepared to discuss that at this stage'	'But we will later'

VERBAL SIGNS

One party says:	And means:
'That's a lot more than our budget'	'So, it had better offer real value and extra benefit'
'It is not our policy to give additional discounts and if we did they would not be as much as 10%'	'Would you accept 5%?'
'Our price for that quantity is X'	'But, for a larger quantity .....'
'They are the standard terms and conditions'	'But we could negotiate'
'It seems like an extremely reasonable arrangement'	'It is best for me'
'It is a good price'	'It is profitable for us'
'I can't say I am happy with the arrangement but .....'	'I agree, but may ask for something else'

INTERPERSONAL BEHAVIOUR

CONTROL THE TEMPERATURE

You negotiate best when pursuing a calm, considered approach.

Do not risk the negotiation collapsing:

- Do not press an issue, especially early on (digging in your heels can create an impasse)
- Keep the range of issues in mind
- Leave difficult points aside to finalise them later

Overall, keep pushing on with the most straightforward issues. Some of the other points will get simpler as overall agreement comes nearer.

BEHAVIOURAL 'PLOYS'

HIDDEN MOTIVES

Icebergs are 9/10ths hidden. Similarly, you say something, ask a question perhaps, and do not seem to get a straight answer. The reason is that the other people are searching for the hidden motives that they are sure lie behind your questions. Agreement is therefore held back for no good reason.

It makes sense to spell out **why** you are doing things – asking a certain question or pursuing a certain line – so that most of what is hidden becomes clear.

Of course, you may have motives that you **want** hidden, at least for the moment. That is OK. But, if the other people think you are being more devious than you are, it will not help matters.

INTERPERSONAL BEHAVIOUR

BEHAVIOURAL 'PLOYS'

FLAGGING (1)

Clear 'flagging' of how you are proceeding shows how the negotiation may progress, e.g.:

- 'May I ask .....?'

- 'Perhaps, I might suggest .....'

- 'I think it might be easier to settle other details if we can agree on ..... first'

But, **never** flag a disagreement.

BEHAVIOURAL 'PLOYS'

FLAGGING (2)

Example

Julie makes a suggestion: 'Perhaps we can aim for completion of stage one by next Friday'.

Mark immediately disagrees: 'No. I think that's far too long'.

Even if Mark can justify his position, Julie will start developing a retaliatory response from the moment she hears the word 'no'. She won't listen to Mark's explanation as she will already be committed to her answer.

What Mark should have done is respond along the lines of: 'That would be ideal, but we agreed the whole project would be finished by the end of the month. Does next Friday leave us enough time for the other stages?'.

This is more likely to prompt thought and discussion. It might lead to a compromise or acceptable alternative.

BEHAVIOURAL 'PLOYS'

SUMMARIES

Good negotiators summarise regularly because it:

- Keeps complexities under control
- Tests progress
- Lets you restate what the other party has said
- Can help gain the initiative
- Can keep the discussion on track
- Can prevent misinterpretation, misunderstanding and subsequent hard feelings

In other words, summarising helps you stay on top.

INTERPERSONAL BEHAVIOUR

BEHAVIOURAL 'PLOYS'

PSYCHOLOGICAL ATTACK

Some things are said or done, not as part of the argument, but psychologically to disadvantage or 'rattle' the other people. Many tactics can be used in this way:

- Playing for time (making a calculation or a phone call)

- Creating a smoke screen of demands (only one of which is important)

- Flattering or coercing

- Venting anger or emotion

- Having (or appearing to have) total fluency with the facts (wondrous mental arithmetic may have been worked out beforehand or just be a guess which sounds authoritative)

- Creating physical discomfort (providing an uncomfortable chair or seating position, or forcing the other person to balance a coffee cup while he/she is trying to take notes)

- Making financial restraints seem irreversible

- Pretending not to understand

INTERPERSONAL BEHAVIOUR

BEHAVIOURAL 'PLOYS'

DEFEND/ATTACK SPIRALS

Because people feel it is not proper to hit someone without warning, disagreement often starts from mild beginnings.

You may say 'I'm not sure about this' or 'I think we should aim for better than that' while gently moving towards a major negative. The other party, sensing what is happening, then begins to prepare a counter argument. Do not give them time to do this.

Good negotiators do not put others on their guard. If it is appropriate to attack, they do so without warning.

BEHAVIOURAL 'PLOYS'

COUNTER PROPOSALS

Suppose you make proposal X and then the other person makes proposal Y. If you automatically think the other party is disagreeing, you won't be receptive and may not consider the alternative properly. Automatically disagreeing may lead to fruitless restatements of positions, with both parties seeing the other as unhelpful and unconstructive.

If the two proposals are not too far apart, keep the discussion focused on the possibility of agreement and don't adopt a negative stance. That will only block progress towards a mutually agreeable compromise.

INTERPERSONAL BEHAVIOUR

BEHAVIOURAL 'PLOYS'

MAINTAINING THE RITUAL

The process of negotiation is, in itself, important. Some negotiators feel cheated if the 'game' is not played out. Therefore:

- Never take the first offer
- Don't make totally unacceptable conditions
- Allow adequate time, especially so that the other party need not rush (though urgency can be a ploy)

Use the whole process rather than attempting to shortcut it.

BEHAVIOURAL 'PLOYS'

FUTURE RELATIONSHIPS

Always aim towards ending on a pleasant note and plan a last move to make that happen. Remember:

- Negotiation does get acrimonious
- Negotiation is adversarial
- Hard bargains need to be driven
- An on-going relationship may be involved so ensure that the way one negotiation ends sets the scene for the next

BEHAVIOURAL 'PLOYS'
ACTIVE LISTENING

Good negotiators listen carefully: the best negotiators miss nothing.

DON'T

✗ Be distracted

✗ Let thoughts of your next move prevent you taking in the current situation

✗ Let emotion put you off (perhaps the other party is **trying** to make you angry)

DO

✔ Double check if necessary

✔ Ask questions as appropriate

✔ Be seen to be giving the matter your undivided attention

Only when you have 100% of the message will you be able to deal with it effectively.

'People were designed with two ears and one mouth, and that is the ratio in which to use them.'

BEHAVIOURAL 'PLOYS'
ACTIVE LISTENING (cont'd)

Beware of hearing what you want to hear.

Do not make assumptions. Remember the old saying:

'Never assume anything; assuming makes an ass out of you and me.'

A S S / U / M E

INTERPERSONAL BEHAVIOUR

BEHAVIOURAL 'PLOYS'
ASKING QUESTIONS

You cannot ask too many questions.

RULE ONE – phrase them carefully
RULE TWO – use 'open' questions

There are two ways of asking questions. One is to ask open-ended questions that do not permit a 'yes' or 'no' answer (e.g.: 'How do you feel about thrashing out the terms and conditions?').

The other more dangerous method is to ask a closed or yes/no question (e.g.: 'Will you negotiate?'). This risks a deadlocking 'No'. Closed questions obtain less information. You risk proceeding with less knowledge.

Open-ended questions are preferable. They allow the other person to develop his or her own answer, not just accept or reject your words. Also, they encourage the other party to talk, which is important, especially at the beginning of a conversation.

You want a dialogue, not a monologue.

BEHAVIOURAL 'PLOYS'
ASKING PROBING QUESTIONS

You must unearth the real reasons, thinking and needs of the other party. So sometimes questions must be used in sequence to probe for information:

- *Background questions* give you basic information from which you can begin to draw conclusions
- *Problem questions* begin to focus on their situation
- *Effect questions* help focus on what is happening as a result of the prevailing situation
- *Need questions* get the person to state needs in their terms

The following, while not exactly representing real life, makes the sequence clear:

Where are you?	Up to my neck in the river
Does this pose any problem?	Yes, I can't swim
So what will happen if you stay there?	I shall probably drown
Do you want me to pull you out?	Yes, please

The first answer poses as many questions as it answers (maybe it is a hot day and the person is swimming). The last is entirely specific and puts the rope salesman on the bank in a powerfully persuasive position!

You will always do better if you find out what the situation really is on the other side.

BEHAVIOURAL 'PLOYS'

BODY LANGUAGE

While some regard it as a pseudo science, body language can be a useful (if not infallible) guide that helps you 'read between the lines'. **Watch** for it and **use** it (perhaps to give a particular impression).

Signs to look for include:

Open mindedness shown by:
- Open hands
- Unbuttoned coat

Wariness shown by:
- Arms crossed on chest
- Legs over chair arm while seated
- Fistlike gestures
- Karate chops
- Crossed legs
- Sitting in armless chair reversed
- Pointing index finger

BEHAVIOURAL 'PLOYS'

BODY LANGUAGE (cont'd)

Thinking/analysing shown by:

- Hand to face gestures
- Stroking chin
- Taking glasses off and cleaning them
- Putting hand to bridge of nose

- Head tilted
- Peering over glasses
- Glasses earpiece in mouth
- Getting up from table and walking

Confidence shown by:

- Steepling of the hands
- Hands on back of head (authoritative position)
- Hands on lapels of coat

- Back stiffened
- Hands in coat pockets, with thumbs outside

INTERPERSONAL BEHAVIOUR

BEHAVIOURAL 'PLOYS'

BODY LANGUAGE (cont'd)

Territorial dominance shown by:

- Feet on desk
- Feet on chair
- Hands behind head and leaning back

- Leaning against/touching object
- Placing object in a desired place

Nervousness shown by:

- Clearing throat
- Whistling
- Picking/pinching skin
- Hands covering mouth while speaking
- Tugging at trousers or skirt while seated
- Perspiration/wringing of hands
- 'Whew' sound

- Fidgeting in chair
- Not looking at the other person
- Jingling money in pockets
- Tugging at ear

BEHAVIOURAL 'PLOYS'

BODY LANGUAGE (cont'd)

Frustration shown by:

- Short breaths
- Tightly clenched hands
- Fistlike gestures
- Running hand through hair
- Tutting sound
- Wringing hands
- Pointing index finger
- Rubbing back of neck

Boredom shown by:

- Doodling
- Blank stare
- Legs crossed/foot kicking
- Drumming
- Head in palms of hands

Acceptance shown by:

- Hand to chest
- Touching gestures
- Open arms and hands
- Moving closer

INTERPERSONAL BEHAVIOUR

BEHAVIOURAL 'PLOYS'

BODY LANGUAGE (cont'd)

Expectancy shown by:

- Rubbing palms
- Crossed fingers
- Jingling money
- Moving closer

Suspicion shown by:

- Not looking at you
- Moving away from you
- Touching/rubbing nose
- Buttoning coat
- Silhouette body towards you
- Arms crossed
- Sideways glance
- Rubbing eye(s)
- Drawing away

Alertness/attention shown by:

- Hands on hips
- Moving closer
- Hand to face gestures
- Hands on mid-thigh when seated
- Arms spread, gripping edge of table/desk
- Sitting on edge of chair
- Open hands
- Unbuttoning coat
- Tilted head

BEHAVIOURAL RESPONSES

THE 'CHAOS' RESPONSE

Next, a series of classic situations and responses, all with the potential to keep you on track.

Line of behaviour taken by other party:

'Chaos': displays anger, storms out

Hoping you will:

Apologise, give concession or get angry yourself

Action

- Keep calm
- Express concern at any misunderstanding
- Seek clarification
- Let things return to normal before trying to proceed

INTERPERSONAL BEHAVIOUR

BEHAVIOURAL RESPONSES

THE 'POOR ME' RESPONSE

Line of behaviour taken by other party:

'Poor me': plea for special sympathy, concern or approach because of their situation

Hoping you will:

Give more because you feel sorry for them

Action

- Do not be put off or be overly sympathetic
- Acknowledge the problem
- Restate your position and take the conversation back on track

BEHAVIOURAL RESPONSES

THE 'NOT ME' RESPONSE

Line of behavioUr taken by other party:

'Not me': claims cannot make decision; must refer to boss, spouse, committee, etc

Hoping this will:

Exert pressure without souring relations ('It is not my fault.')

Action

- Ask questions designed to ascertain whether what is said is true or just a ploy
- In some meetings it may be an aspect worth checking early on: 'Do you have the authority to make an arrangement or should we involve someone else?'

BEHAVIOURAL RESPONSES

THE 'ONLY OPTION' RESPONSE

Line of behaviour taken by other party:

'Only option': keeps suggesting unacceptable option without alternative

Hoping you will:

Be forced into agreement, seeing no option

Action

- Keep calm
- Bear your objectives firmly in mind
- Suggest other alternatives or perhaps middle ground
- Keep explaining why their option is not feasible

89

BEHAVIOURAL RESPONSES

THE 'NO WAY' RESPONSE

Line of behaviour taken by other party:

'No way': immediately states one element as non-negotiable

Hoping you will:

Give up or offer a great deal to try to make it negotiable

Action

- Offer to set that element aside, moving on to other things and getting back to it once rapport is established and agreement is clear on some other elements

BEHAVIOURAL RESPONSES

THE 'WHAT' RESPONSE

Line of behaviour taken by other party:

'What': over-reaction to something (shock, horror) to indicate impasse

Hoping you will:

Offer a rapid concession to compensate

Action

- Ignore the first response and restate the issue to prompt a more considered, informative response

BEHAVIOURAL RESPONSES

THE 'CAN'T' RESPONSE

Line of behaviour taken by other party:

'Can't': opens with a problem ('Of course, we can't do anything unless the project can be completed by the end of the month')

Hoping you will:

Concede

Action

- Question to establish truth – this may just be an opening stance
- Refer to the other variables

INTERPERSONAL BEHAVIOUR

BEHAVIOURAL RESPONSES

THE 'NO-CAN-DO' RESPONSE

Line of behaviour taken by other party:

'No-Can-Do': a comment that contains no detail/reason but is very negative ('That's just not at all acceptable')

Hoping you will:

See it as intractable and give in

Action

- Ask for detail ('Why is it unacceptable? How different does it need to be?')
- Get away from the non-specific and down to the facts of the argument

INTERPERSONAL BEHAVIOUR

BEHAVIOURAL RESPONSES

THE 'SOMETHING MORE' RESPONSE

Line of behaviour taken by other party:

'Something more': an out and out request for some extra benefit

Hoping you will:

Give it to gain goodwill and keep things going

Action

- Investigate the trading possibilities ('If I give you X, would you be able to agree to Y?')

INTERPERSONAL BEHAVIOUR

BEHAVIOURAL RESPONSES

THE 'POLICY' RESPONSE

Line of behaviour taken by other party:	*Hoping you will:*
'Policy': the 'rules' are quoted ('More than my job's worth') – company policy	Read it as unchangeable and not even try to negotiate

Action

- Check whether it is true, whether there are exceptions, whether others have authority to make exceptions
- Rules are made to be broken but be prepared for this to be difficult on occasion and, if necessary, be prepared to accept them

INTERPERSONAL BEHAVIOUR

BEHAVIOURAL RESPONSES

THE 'SELL ME' RESPONSE

Line of behaviour taken by other party:

'Sell me': negotiation is dependent on a tacit agreement (e.g.: to buy, to action); if the deal itself is put in question the whole situation may be changing

Hoping you will:

Give in to secure agreement

Action

- Ask yourself 'Should I go back to the stage of persuasion or is it a ploy?' If it is a ploy, stick to your position, continue to negotiate, and push back hard

INTERPERSONAL BEHAVIOUR

BEHAVIOURAL RESPONSES

THE 'BIG vs LITTLE' RESPONSE

Line of behaviour taken by other party:

'Big vs Little': a big deal is made of a small point, then used as a concession for something really wanted

Hoping you will:

See the first as a real issue and trade, in a way that is not a good exchange

Action

- Check real importance
- Compare and deal with the two things together

BEHAVIOURAL RESPONSES

THE 'NO PROGRESS' RESPONSE

Line of behaviour taken by other party:	*Hoping you will:*
'No progress': things appear to be deadlocked, no clear way out	See your giving in as the only way forward

Action

- Suggest a real change, a break, an arbitrator (if it is a ploy these may be resisted and you can get back on track)

BEHAVIOURAL RESPONSES

'FINE TUNING'

The whole process of negotiation needs a 'sensitive hand on the tiller'.

You need constantly to react – to what you expected as a response or action from the other party – and to be quick on your feet, responding to the unexpected.

Such responses must be **prompt** yet **considered**. Avoiding over-reaction, keep yourself on the course you set.

BEHAVIOURAL RESPONSES
LEARNING FROM EXPERIENCE

The behavioural response possibilities are almost infinite.

Observe everything that occurs, monitor what works for you and **keep notes.**

Use your notes when preparing for your next negotiating meeting.

SUMMARY CHECKLISTS

CHECKLIST 1

PRINCIPLES OF NEGOTIATION

1. **Definition: negotiation is about bargaining to reach a mutually agreeable outcome**
   This is the 'win-win' concept.
2. **Never neglect your preparation**
   Have a clear plan (but remain flexible).
3. **Participants must regard each other as equals**
   Mutual respect is essential to both conduct and outcome.
4. **There is a need to 'abide by the rules'**
   Negotiation is about discussion, rather than debate. There is little place for overt
   one-upmanship or domination, yet each must fight their corner.
5. **Put your cards on the table**
   At least on major issues, do not mislead or state intentions that are simply untrue.
6. **Patience is a key characteristic of the good negotiator**
   Take your time. Do not rush discussion or decision-making. Delay is better than a poor
   outcome.

CHECKLIST 1

PRINCIPLES OF NEGOTIATION (cont'd)

7. **Empathy is vital**
   Put yourself in the other person's shoes. See things from their point of view and do so objectively.

8. **State clear objectives**
   Being open, early on, about overall intentions can save 'groping in the dark'.

9. **Avoid confrontation**
   Do not get into a corner that you cannot get out of. Avoid arguments and showdowns but stand firm and keep calm.

10. **Position disagreement carefully**
    Act as devil's advocate (looking at the case from the other person's viewpoint) to avoid a confrontational 'I disagree' style.

11. **Deal with concessions progressively**
    Where concessions have to be made, make them unwillingly and one at a time – and trade them.

12. **Do not let perfection be the enemy of the good**
    An outcome that is 100% what you want is rarely (if ever) an option. Be realistic and do not waste time and effort seeking something out of reach.

CHECKLIST 1

PRINCIPLES OF NEGOTIATION (cont'd)

13. Be open (but not totally)
Declaring your plans, intentions may be useful to the discussion. However, you may want to hide your motivations or priorities.

14. Stick with your objectives
Aim high and settle as high as possible. Know when to drop the whole thing rather than agree to a totally inappropriate deal.

15. Keep on your guard
Maintain your stamina and bide your time. The other party may persevere for hours to see when you will crack.

16. Remain 'professional'
For example, respect confidences that are given in the course of negotiations. Such consideration builds relationships and may help you next time.

17. Never underestimate people
A velvet glove may be disguising an iron fist.

18. End positively
Neither party will get exactly what they want, but if the deal is agreeable emphasise this agreement at the end.

CHECKLIST 2

TACTICS OF NEGOTIATION

1. **Select the right starting point**
   Your plan should make it easy for you to take the initiative and get quickly onto your agenda.

2. **Aim high**
   This way the trading moves you less far from what you regard as a good position.

3. **Do not make your feelings obvious**
   There is an element of bluff. If your face (and body language) say 'this is minor' as you respond to something major you will be better off.

4. **Use silence**
   Some things demand no reaction at all.

5. **Watch for early difficulty**
   Let a rapport and momentum build up before you tackle contentious issues.

6. **Do not exaggerate facts**
   They can be verified and cause problems later.

CHECKLIST 2

TACTICS OF NEGOTIATION (cont'd)

7. **Communicate clearly**
   Remember the need for understanding as a foundation to the whole process.

8. **Be seen to go with the other person's way of doing things**
   Do this at least to some degree, and particularly if you are on 'their ground'.

9. **Do not push too hard**
   There is usually a line beyond which the outcome is not a better deal but a complete breakdown.

10. **When negotiation is finished, stop**
    Once agreement is reached, is clear, agreed upon and perhaps noted, move on to other matters so that you do not find people saying 'You know I have been thinking …..' In that case you are back to square one.

SUMMARY CHECKLISTS

CHECKLIST 3
SOME FINAL DON'TS

✗ Don't overreact
✗ Don't become emotional
✗ Don't lose patience
✗ Don't be unpleasant
✗ Don't be provocative
✗ Don't be insulting
✗ Don't push too hard

The only exceptions to these are on a **very controlled basis** when, for instance, a situation calls for a brief display of impatience.

Never agree to something you do not want. Bear in mind your 'minimum deal' requirement. It is sometimes better to walk away.

SUMMARY CHECKLISTS

LAST WORD

Negotiation is a social skill. Ultimately the only way to refine your technique is to do it, note what happens, and do it again and again. Practice makes perfect.

So, put all your cards on the table .....

On second thoughts .....

About the Author

Patrick Forsyth
Patrick runs Touchstone Training &
Consultancy, an independent firm
specialising in marketing, management and
communications skills training. He began his
career in publishing and worked for a professional
management institute before going into consultancy. He
started his own firm in 1990. He has worked widely in many
different industries and internationally. Writing is a key part of
his work. He has more than fifty successful business books
published including *Successful Time Management, Marketing
Professional Services* and *Managing in the Discomfort Zone*,
and his writing has been well reviewed: *hugely readable and
practical* (in 'Professional Marketing' magazine). He also
writes corporate publications. He has written several other
pocketbooks: *Sales Excellence, Meetings, Managing
Upwards,* and *Starting in Management*.

Contact
Touchstone Training & Consultancy, 28 Saltcote Maltings,
Maldon, Essex CM9 4QP United Kingdom.
patrick@touchstonetc.freeserve.co.uk

MANAGEMENT
POCKETBOOKS

Published by:
Management Pocketbooks Ltd,
Laurel House, Station Approach,
Alresford, Hants S024 9JH UK

© Patrick Forsyth 1993, 2000.
All rights reserved.

First edition published 1993.
This edition published 2000.
Reprinted 2001, 2003, 2004, 2006.

ISBN-13 978 1 870471 84 8
ISBN-10 1 870471 84 9

Design, typesetting and graphics
by **efex ltd**. Printed in UK

British Library Cataloguing-in-
Publication Data – a catalogue
record for this book is available
from the British Library.

ORDER FORM

Your details

Name _____

Position _____

Company _____

Address _____

_____

Telephone _____

Fax _____

E-mail _____

VAT No. (EC companies) _____

Your Order Ref _____

Please send me:

		No. copies
The Negotiators	Pocketbook	
The _____	Pocketbook	
The _____	Pocketbook	
The _____	Pocketbook	
The _____	Pocketbook	

Order by Post

MANAGEMENT POCKETBOOKS LTD

LAUREL HOUSE, STATION APPROACH,
ALRESFORD, HAMPSHIRE SO24 9JH UK

Order by Phone, Fax or Internet

Telephone: +44 (0)1962 735573
Facsimile: +44 (0)1962 733637
E-mail: sales@pocketbook.co.uk
Web: www.pocketbook.co.uk

MANAGEMENT POCKETBOOKS